HOW MONEY WORKS

COUNTRY MONEY

By William Whitehead, Felicia Law and Gerry Bailey
Illustrated by Mark Beech

NORWOOD HOUSE PRESS
Chicago, Illinois

NORWOOD HOUSE  PRESS

P.O. Box 316598 · Chicago, Illinois 60631
For more information about Norwood House Press please visit our website at
www.norwoodhousepress.com or call 866-565-2900.

LIBRARY OF CONGRESS CATALOGING-IN-PUBLICATION DATA
    Whitehead, William, 1942-
     Country money / written by William Whitehead, Felicia Law & Gerry Bailey.
       pages cm. -- (How money works)
     Illustrated by Mark Beech.
     Includes index.
     Summary: "Presents an introduction to financial literacy and the factors that affect a country's economy, such as natural
resources, population, geography, climate, wealth, and more. Includes index, glossary, and discussion questions"-- Provided
by publisher.
     ISBN 978-1-59953-719-1 (library edition : alk. paper) -- ISBN 978-1-60357-822-6 (ebook)
    1. Money--Juvenile literature. 2. Economics--Juvenile literature. 3. Wealth--Juvenile literature. I. Law, Felicia. II. Bailey, Gerry,
1945- III. Beech, Mark, 1971- illustrator. IV. Title.
    HG221.5.W484 2015
    330--dc23
             2015003657

274N – 062015
Manufactured in the United States of America in North Mankato, Minnesota.

COUNTRY MONEY

HOW COUNTRIES SPEND THEIR MONEY – AND WHY

Contents

Words that appear in red throughout the text are
defined in the glossary on pages 62-63.

A Country and Its Money

You almost certainly know quite a lot about needing money. You see it being spent by adults in your family when they need to buy food or gas, or even pay bills to the electricity or water companies. And you know exactly how your allowance is spent – or saved – or whatever you need to do with it. But your country – the one you live in – needs money, too. And it needs quite a lot!

Large or Small

Every country needs a different amount because it may be large or small. The larger the country, the more it probably needs. But it may be a large country and not have so many cities and towns and people living in it. Equally, it may be small, even an island country, but be crowded with folks.

The money a country needs is all about how much money it takes to make things 'work' for the people who live there.

Making things work

To make things 'work' in a country, money must be spent on lots of different things. People need to be able to move about, so roads and railways and airports must be built to link them all together. Goods made in factories or on farms need to be moved, so ports and rivers are also important.

People need to be educated in schools and colleges, and taken care of when they are old or sick or in need of special care.

Laws are made to protect people and their property. Policemen are needed for control, then courts of law to judge crimes, and prisons where those found guilty will be punished.

And perhaps the country needs an army to protect its borders - or even to help another country do the same.

Then it needs people to manage and help run each activity, and offices where they can work, and a large government building where meetings can take place ...

... the list goes on.

Why Countries Need Money

Not all countries spend their money in the same way, but these are some of the things that national or local governments must spend money on.

Social Programs

Social programs include many services that provide care and assistance to people. This can include pensions or retirement funds for retired and disabled people. It can also include unemployment funds and other financial assistance for those in need.

Education

Most countries put education at the top of their 'must have' list. Educating everyone is a costly business. Schools must be built with all the materials and equipment needed. Teachers must be trained and paid.

Industry, Agriculture, Employment

Governments like to see as many people employed as possible. They may give money as grants for training or subsidies to help farmers grow certain crops. They may help the industry by reducing taxes or supporting new building and development.

Law and Order

We all like to feel safe when we're out and about. Countries usually set up police forces at several levels to make sure you're as safe as it's possible to be. Money is needed to pay for the police, their offices, transportation, and training.

Healthcare

We all get sick sometimes and may need to visit a doctor or hospital. In many countries, a healthcare program pays all, or part, of the cost of hospitals, clinics, and the nurses and doctors that work in them, as well as the high-tech equipment that is used. In some cases the cost of drugs is covered, too.

Defense

Each country defends its borders, particularly if it has a neighbor who is aggressive. This means funding a military. Defense can be one of the most expensive things a government must pay for, as it has to buy modern weapons, ships, and planes.

H⊛using

One of the biggest problems a government faces is to provide enough housing for growing populations. This may mean helping local governments create low-cost homes.

Transp⊛rtati⊛n

In order for a country to work efficiently, goods and people must be able to travel from place to place. This means making sure that roads, railroads, and airports are all built.

Debt interest

Governments get most of their money from taxes paid by the people who live and work in the country. But this isn't always enough to pay for everything. They have to borrow money from banks and pay a fee, or interest, on the loan, or debt. The repayments and the interest together can add up to a lot.

BILLIONS

When you count your money, you're probably counting in ones, maybe in tens if you've been saving – and even in hundreds if you've had a birthday celebration! Parents count the family income and expenditure in thousands. But your country operates in hundreds of thousands, in millions, billions, and even occasionally in TRILLIONS!

A billion

What does a billion dollars look like? Well, the photo on the right shows a pile of 1 billion U.S. dollars, so one trillion would be a thousand times bigger!

Here's the math:
* ✳ 100   a hundred
* ✳ 1,000   a thousand   (10 times bigger)
* ✳ 1,000,000   a million   (One million is a thousand thousands)
* ✳ 1,000,000,000   a billion   (One billion is a thousand millions)
* ✳ 1,000,000,000,000   a trillion   (One trillion is a thousand billions)

A trillion

One trillion pennies stacked on top of each other would make a tower about 840,000 miles (1,351,849km) high – the same distance as going to the Moon, back to Earth, then to the Moon again.

Spreading it Out

A country that wants to pay for all these services is going to need a great deal of money.

In the U.S., for example, the government spends about $3.8 trillion on all the things it considers important. That's an incredible amount of money!

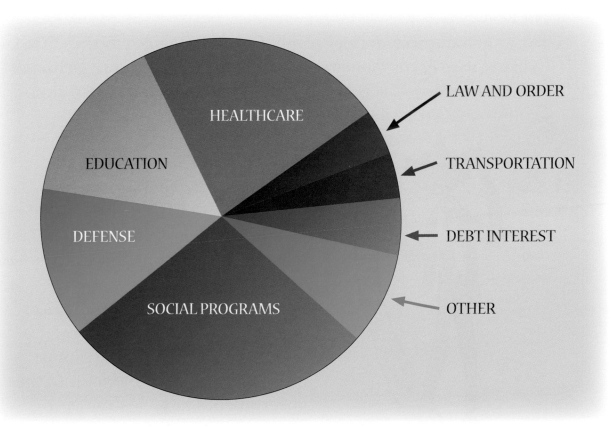

So Where Does it Come From?

Raising the money

Perhaps you think that a government can just print the money it needs whenever it wants to. Someone just sets the printing press going and out it comes. Unfortunately for most governments, it isn't nearly this easy. They rely on everyone to help them. And here's how ...

Taxes

Most of a country's money comes from the people who live in it. Every person who earns money in any form at all is subject to give a portion of this money to the government. It's known as tax, and in almost all countries it's a legal requirement. You HAVE to pay!

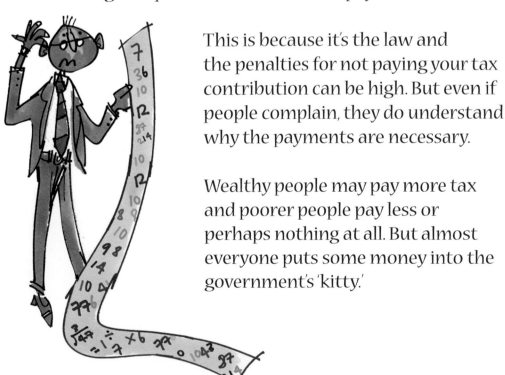

This is because it's the law and the penalties for not paying your tax contribution can be high. But even if people complain, they do understand why the payments are necessary.

Wealthy people may pay more tax and poorer people pay less or perhaps nothing at all. But almost everyone puts some money into the government's 'kitty.'

And more taxes

There are lots of ways to collect taxes. Income tax is collected from people's salaries or other money they earn.

But taxes can be added to all kinds of services, too – and even to the goods you buy.

A tax sometimes called 'Sales' or 'Value Added Tax' is an amount the government or state adds to the price of goods and services. These are goods sold in stores or bills sent in for repairs or other work.

A tax can be added to special kinds of food or drink, especially those that are luxuries and not considered essential to people's health.

Many governments tax gas and cars, and even air flights. The tax is used to try and cut down on air pollution and repair highways.

Taxation's not new!

The Incas were ancient people who lived in the Andes mountains of South America. Inca tribes were only discovered during the Spanish conquest of Peru during the 16th century. The Incas managed very nicely without money.

Money, as such, only existed in the form of work. Each person paid 'taxes' by working on the roads, fields, irrigation canals, temples, and fortresses. In return, Inca rulers paid their laborers in clothing and food. Silver and gold were readily available, but only used for display – not money.

WHO RUNS A COUNTRY?

A country is made up of lots of families. Thousands, sometimes millions of them. A country is not just a king or queen. It's not just a president or a government. It's lots and lots of people living in family groups. And the country must be run so they can all function.

Who's in charge?

Of course, there are far too many people to all run the country together. So someone has to be in charge! Someone has to make sure that things work in every part of the country and not just in one or two places.

For example, they have to make sure that children who live in the countryside have schools to attend as well as those who live in the cities.

i'm boss!

In some countries, there is a ruler who has a lot of power. Or perhaps it's a president who holds the power. Or a rich family. These people will decide how others live and work. They will decide what kind of economy operates in their country. They will decide who pays taxes and how the taxes are spent.

Elected

In countries known as democracies, the population chooses a group of people who will make the decisions on their behalf. This group is elected to power, and everyone else agrees to follow the rules and laws that they lay down. The group is known as the government and they do this work for as long as they are elected.

Each member of a government pays special attention to the needs of the group of people who elected them. Then they also take on the work of supervising the country's general needs.

The Money Boss

One person in the government is given the job of looking after the country's money. In some countries he or she is known as the Finance Minister, and in others, the Treasury Secretary. This is a very important position.

This person is responsible for formulating economic policies on the country's finances, including taxes and debt.

And these will vary from country to country.

PAYING TAXES

Taxes can vary according to where you live. Although most governments try to stay popular by not taking too much tax from businesses and the workforce, there are governments who take no tax at all!

The Rich Pay Most

In most countries, the more you earn, the more tax you pay. It's generally believed that the more you earn, the more you're able to contribute to the country's upkeep.

Governments figure out how much you have to pay by creating a system of rates for different amounts of income. Everyone who's earning a certain amount pays the lowest rate – say, 25% of their earnings. Earn more and a higher rate is paid – perhaps 40%. And sometimes there is a higher rate still.

The Poor Pay Least

The less you earn, the less tax you pay. And in many countries you don't begin to pay tax until you earn a certain amount.

A government may set what is known as a tax threshold. Everyone can earn this amount without having to pay tax. Governments can raise or lower the tax threshold to try and ease poverty.

The Rich Pay Zero!

High levels of taxation may drive the rich out of a country. They move where taxes are lower or where taxes hardly exist at all. These places are called tax havens. Examples include Luxembourg and the Cayman Islands. These economies can survive because the government raises money from taxes on goods, such as import taxes on cars. They may also not need as much money to operate as some other countries.

Everyone Pays!

Denmark is the country with the highest income tax, which is about 61%. The tax code in Denmark is very complicated, with income taxes, work taxes, sales taxes, taxes on 'luxury items,' and various taxes that businesses must pay as a percentage of their salaries. In return for these high taxes, the Danes receive free healthcare and free higher education.

Tax collectors

Of course, taxes don't collect themselves, so there's a whole army of people employed by governments and other authorities to administer and collect taxes. And it's their job to make sure people pay the right amount of tax.

The main job of a tax officer is to oversee the tax programs of the government. This involves the processing of tax returns and claims, the registration of people and companies for tax purposes, and the accounting procedures to be undertaken. So it's a big job.

And there are lots of rules, so tax officers must know about tax law. They need to evaluate information, interpret the law, investigate problems with tax returns and claims, and then solve them.

TAKING A GAMBLE

Governments sometimes find other ways of raising money from the people. They use schemes that are more like games, although they often help a good cause, too.

Lotteries

Lotteries are simple ways of raising money by selling numbered tickets. Any amount of tickets can be sold, and on a given day there is a drawing. The holder of the drawn ticket wins a prize. The rest of the money is used to help pay for education or some other cost or, perhaps, a charity.

Some people object to lotteries because they see them as a form of gambling. But others consider them just a bit of fun to be had for a good cause.

National lotteries are held in many countries. They are generally set up to support a number of good causes. The largest win recorded in the United States saw three tickets win $656 million in 2014.

Government bonds

The government may raise money by asking people to invest in it. It may issue bonds, which are simply notes that promise to pay you all your money back, with interest, at an agreed upon time.

These bonds help raise money to finance special projects.

Printing money

Zimbabwe is one of Africa's poorest countries. It saw many years of poor government fiscal policy. Industry slowed, agriculture failed, and while people in the country starved or earned just a few cents a month, exports fell. Even today, some estimate the unemployment rate there is 95% of the population.

In 2006, the value of the currency began to fall further. But `borrowing' in Zimbabwe - or printing money - just went on until it was out of control. Soon the money had little value.

And three years later, in 2009, the Zimbabwean dollar was worthless and was abolished altogether.

This hundred trillion dollar note was issued in Zimbabwe.

Country to Country

You probably know what your own currency will buy in a local store. You use it to buy goods that you need or want. But money can be bought and sold for itself – just as any other kind of goods – like sugar or shoes. There are people whose job it is to buy and sell your country's currency. Indeed, all day long, people all over the planet are buying and selling each other's currencies.

★oreign exchange

How much you pay for a country's currency is called the exchange rate. Currencies are bought and sold on the foreign exchange market, which is the biggest money market in the world.

Coming to stay

When someone comes to your country from abroad, they can't use their own currency to buy things in your stores. Let's say they come from France and are visiting the U.S. They'll need to use the foreign exchange market to buy U.S. dollars. And they'll pay for them using euros, the currency of France, at a certain exchange rate.

Exchange rate

The exchange rate is the rate at which one currency can be exchanged for another. It's how much you pay to buy some of another nation's currency.

How much you pay depends on the value of the currency you are buying compared to the value of your own.

You have to take into account two currencies – your currency and the foreign currency. If you go to a bank, a travel agent, or a specialist exchange bureau, you can usually see a list of the prices charged in your currency for a number of foreign currencies.

floating OR Fixed

Exchange rates can be floating or fixed. With floating rates the rate depends upon how much people want and are willing to pay for a certain currency. Most countries use a floating exchange rate.

A fixed rate means that a currency is fixed to another popular currency. The second currency goes up or down in value when the original currency goes up and down in value.

Two prices

Normally there are two prices listed. One price is how much you have to pay if you're buying a certain currency, while the second is how much you'll receive if you're selling instead.

Usually you lose value if you're selling a currency anywhere but in its home country.

COUNTRY CASH

What's your currency called? Here are just some of the world's countries and their currency names.

Afghan afghani
Albanian lek
Algerian dinar
Argentine peso
Australian dollar
Azerbaijani manat
Bangladeshi taka
Bhutanese ngultrum
Brazilian real
British pound
Bulgarian lev
Canadian dollar
Chilean peso
Chinese yuan renminbi
Croatian kuna
Czech koruna
Danish krone
Hungarian forint
Icelandic króna
Indian rupee
Indonesian rupiah

Iranian rial
Iraqi dinar
Japanese yen
Malaysian ringgit
Mexican peso
Moroccan dirham
Norwegian kroner
Pakistani rupee
Philippine peso
Romanian leu
Saudi riyal
South African rand
South Korean won
Swedish krona
Swiss franc
Taiwan dollar
Thai baht
Turkish lira
Ukrainian hryvnia
United States dollar
Vietnamese dong

Making coins

The manufacture of coins is called minting. At first, no one trusted that the value of a coin was genuine, so the rulers in each country allowed their head to be stamped on them.

Every coin comes from a currency-making factory called a mint. Each country 'mints' its own coins.

All coins begin as a metal strip 13 inches wide and 1,500 feet long (33cm x 457m). The strips are wound into coils, then fed into a blanking press. This punches out round discs of metal called blanks. The blanks are heated and softened in a furnace. Then they pass through a heater and dryer. This preparation also makes them shiny.

The next stage is to add the design and lettering. This process is called striking. The blanks are passed through a press that strikes, or presses, the amount, words, and pictures onto them.

Making bills

Bills have to be made so people can't forge them easily. There's a lot of secrecy about how they're actually produced.

For security, bills are printed on paper that's made from cotton fibers. The paper also contains a special kind of thread that can't be photocopied.

The artist's design is engraved onto a steel plate called an intaglio plate. When ink is applied to a plate, it fills in the lines and marks.

Specially-mixed inks are used to apply invisible, secret features onto each bill. This means that banks and stores can use special lights to detect forgeries.

Most bills have a watermark design that is molded into the paper. Often, the security thread appears and disappears between the bars of the watermark.

A Country and Its Economy

The economy is a grand-sounding word for all the activity that goes on in a country. It's a word that sums up every small sale and purchase in every store, every hour of work done in offices and factories, every movement of goods in and out of a warehouse ... in fact, every piece of business going on anywhere.

It starts at home

When adults go to work in the morning, they become part of the economy. They will spend their day making the products or producing the services that help the country's businesses to run.

In return, they will receive money for them and their family to live on. The family money will buy products and services that the family needs. This is known as consumer spending.

In this way, the money moves on to other businesses and services. It is kept in circulation.

It moves, it earns, and it grows.

A good economy

Governments try hard to keep the economy active. They want the money to move around and keep a lot of businesses and people working hard and spending. They want high demand for goods and services, and need everyone to build products and provide services at a rapid rate.

Why? A bustling economy means that people are working and can buy the things they need. It also means that companies are paying taxes to the government on their profits. It means workers are paying taxes on their wages. And all these taxes are supplying services – roads, education, medical services, and so on.

A poor economy

A poor economy happens when demand is not as great. Fewer goods and services are needed and produced. Factories start to make less. Work hours are shortened and people may lose their jobs altogether. They have less money to spend, so stores suffer, too.

Taxable income falls and the government has less and less to spend.

I am an economist

It seems obvious, but an economist is someone who studies an economy and tries to predict what will happen. This is a job for people who like sorting out financial problems and coming up with their own theories.

The work covers a lot of things, such as the finances associated with natural resources, consumer spending, distribution of goods and services, energy costs, bank interest rates, and international as well as national trade.

Economists advise businesses, banks, governments, and other organizations on what economic policy to adopt. They use mathematics to predict what will happen if these steps are taken by an organization.

GDP

Around the world, there are countries with bustling, active economies and many that have slower ones. The wealthiest economies are those that trade successfully with other countries. Perhaps they sell raw materials, also known as commodities, such as iron and timber, or they sell other products and even the particular skills of their people.

How big?

The size of a country's economy is measured by adding up the total money value of all the work that is done by the citizens of a country in a single year. This includes all the products that are made and all the services that are produced.

Every small detail is known and counted. Economists add up the sales value of T-shirts sewn in a factory or medical payments made for a sick child. They add the sales of airline tickets and grocery payments – millions and millions of transactions like these. Added up, they produce a grand total.

Average earnings

This grand total is then divided by the number of working people living in the country. This produces a figure showing what the average individual has contributed to the country's overall wealth – or has earned – in any year. The measurement is known as the Gross Domestic Product or GDP.

Having a Share

A country that is producing and selling is almost certainly growing its GDP. People are getting wealthier and business are becoming more prosperous.

In a prosperous, confident country, many people will support factories and other businesses by investing in them. They lend the companies money to grow and expand by buying a small part, known as a share. If the companies make a profit, they share this with all those investors who lent them money, known as their shareholders.

Inflation

Over a period of time, the price of just about everything goes up. This means that in twenty years, $10 won't buy nearly as much as it does today. This general increase in the cost of things over time is known as inflation.

Governments try hard to keep inflation low. They don't want prices rising so high that people have to spend more and more on basic essentials, leaving them less money to live. Rising prices tend to make people unhappy, and governments are chosen and elected because they make people happy – not unhappy!

Inflation can be controlled if the government passes laws to stop price rises, or if it reduces taxes on certain goods, or if it contributes money – known as a subsidy – toward the cost.

BUMPS IN THE ROAD

It may seem odd, but just like you or your family, a country can lose money. If it doesn't earn as much money as it spends, then it experiences what economists call a budget deficit. This means it can't pay for all the things it needs to pay for. And if this goes on for too long, a country can get into real debt and difficulty.

Slump

A slump is when an economy, industry, or market performs poorly. It also refers to a slowdown in business activity. When the market hits a slump, for instance, share prices and share investment both go down.

CLOSED

Recession

A recession happens when the slowdown in the economy lasts longer than 6 months. It affects industry, employment, people's income, and all trade.

Recessions can be caused by risky investment strategies used by financial institutions such as banks. It can harm the economies of both the world's developed and developing countries.

In 2008, American investors placed such high values on real estate that they became too high – and led to an economic crash of the real estate market.

The Great Depression

In 1928, the future looked bright. The American economy was in a healthy state and investors were urged to spend and invest.

Many people were trying to get rich quick. Then came 1929 – and the party was over. On October 24th, 'Black Thursday,' the stock market crashed. Overall, the value of business investments went down by $25 billion. Many investors lost everything and the Great Depression followed.

Hundreds of thousands of people lost their jobs and lined up for help from the government. It took ten years of suffering before confidence was restored and people could find work easily again.

OUt ⊛F W⊛RK

Working at something that has a purpose is an essential human need. Work is supposed to make us feel that we are contributing, being useful, and earning our place on the planet. We are also made to feel that we're somehow failing if we're not working.

Unfortunately, no country can guarantee jobs for everyone. There are over 7 billion people in the world, with 3 billion in the workforce. Of those, 205 million people are considered unemployed. Unemployed people can be found even in the richest countries in North America and Europe.

Factors That Influence a Country's Economy

What makes countries different? What makes one country seem wealthier or more crowded or more beautiful or historic than another? Why do people want to live in some countries and not in others? What are the influences that make countries so different?

Geography

A country with fewer physical barriers, mountains, deserts, volcanoes, lakes, and so on, is easier to travel in. People and goods can move more freely to work and trade with each other.

Climate

Climate describes the weather that is typical to a particular region. A moderate climate – not too hot or cold with enough rainfall to keep water supplies flowing – is a great help to a country. Money is not needed for extra heating or cooling of homes or businesses, and water helps grow crops to feed the people.

Natural Resources

What lies hidden below the ground is often a key to how successful a country can become. Fuels such as coal and oil, or metals and minerals such as aluminium or gold, can be sold to other countries and create wealth.

Agriculture

Central to a country's economic success is its ability to provide food for its citizens. A country with ample farmland to grow and sell crops will be at an advantage over countries that cannot.

Goods & Services

Factories make products. They use materials that can be found locally if possible, as these will be easier to get and probably cheaper. Services are not as easy to see as products, but they help make people's lives more comfortable and successful.

Neighbors

Modern, successful countries often have a long history of trade, of travel, and friendship with other neighboring countries.

Education

Getting educated is about becoming a person with ideas and imagination. It's about having the skills to make and create. A country that invests in education for all its people will almost certainly prosper more than one that doesn't.

Labor

How hard people work tends to vary from country to country. Those who work hard are said to have a good work ethic.

Population

Countries need to balance their population numbers with the amount of natural resources, jobs, and food available.

Technology

Technology requires higher education and skilled workers. When combined with a manufacturing base and products to export, technology plays a great role in a country's economic prospects.

INFLUENCES: Geography

Geography, the position of a country and the kind of land it has, can make a difference to how successful it is. People and goods need to move, so transport by land, sea, and air, is helpful. When mountains, canyons, or deserts get in the way of this, or there are few roads or seaports, trade becomes difficult.

C⊛asts

Countries with a border on a sea or ocean can develop ports from which its goods can be sent around the world. In the 16th century, coastal countries such as Spain, Portugal, Italy, and Britain, became wealthy through shipping and trade. Today, new ports in Asia and the U.S. among others, service loaded container ships carrying all kinds of goods in and out.

Mountain ranges form a natural barrier between countries.

M⊛untains

When a country has a mountainous border, it becomes more difficult to move from place to place and trade with neighboring countries.

Deserts

Some countries are made up of mostly desert. Here, it's difficult to grow crops and people can go hungry. Deserts are also difficult to cross, the population is low, and industry and trade are limited.

A desert can be the size of a large country.

RIVERS

Rivers form a natural border, as they may need long bridges to cross. But they can also be used to transport goods cheaply.

Lakes

Several countries may border a lake. The string of the five Great Lakes forms a natural border between the U.S. and Canada, for example.

FORESTS

Forests can be thick and so tangled that they are impossible to move through. Cambodia is a heavily forested country that shares forest borders with Thailand, Laos, and Vietnam. These countries are now working together to stop illegal cutting of valuable Siamese rosewood trees.

• • • • • • • • • • • • • • • • • • • •

BORDERS as barriers

Of course, all these geographical features can be used as natural borders, separating one country from another. But some borders are man-made. They exist to keep people apart, to protect them from each other's beliefs, language, culture, or politics. Such borders also completely block trade between neighbors.

A wire fence separates Israel and Palestine.

INFLUENCES: Climate

Climate is not the same as weather. Weather is what happens from day to day. It includes the temperature, how much rainfall there will be, the strength of the wind, and other factors as well such as air pressure. Climate is how weather systems behave over a long period of time.

Zones

Different climates exist in different zones on Earth and have specific names. Tropical climates, for example, occur around the equator where there are few temperature extremes. Here it is usually hot, unlike areas to the north and south.

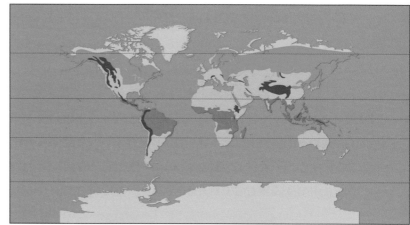

temperate   tropical   desert   mountain   cold   polar

Rice farmers flood their fields for planting after the seasonal monsoon rains.

planting weather

The climate zone in which a country exists can have an influence on its economy, especially if its economy is based on agriculture. Farmers rely on the seasons to bring certain kinds of weather to help crops grow.

Typhoons and hurricanes bring strong winds, floods, and damage.

Droughts kill crops and dry up vital water supplies for people.

A hurricane, viewed from a space satellite, can be seen swirling above the land.

Damaging Weather

If there is a drought, crops will suffer. The lack of water will damage growth, so there will be less to harvest. As a result, there will be less food to go around and prices will go up. A change in weather patterns can also encourage infectious diseases in plants, cause monsoons, prevent crops from being harvested, or at worst, destroy an entire crop.

Changing Climate

Today, most scientists agree that our planet is warming up. Glaciers are shrinking, the Arctic ice is melting, sea levels are rising, and storms are more violent. Droughts are more severe, and storms are more destructive. Some scientists say that it is humans who have caused this to happen. Every day we burn coal and oil – also known as fossil fuels – and the fumes from these fuels have increased gases that shield the Earth from normal cooling in a "greenhouse" effect.

Burning fossil fuels creates a "greenhouse" effect.

INFLUENCES: Natural Resources

Some countries have access to natural resources such as oil, gas, iron ore, or coal within their own borders. They can mine these from the ground, or in some cases, they can move it where it's needed or use it to power machinery.

Forests provide timber for building, but can be destroyed too fast.

RESOURCES ARE POWER

However, those countries without natural resources have to rely on trade with countries that do have them in order to develop. They have to buy what they don't have.

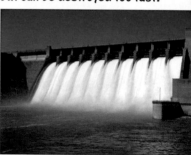

Water is essential for homes, businesses, and farming.

This can cause problems because the countries with the natural resources can say how much they will cost and how much they might be willing to sell. They can raise prices in order to help their own economy, but this may damage the economy of other countries that rely on them.

Mining and tunneling through rock provides for metals and minerals.

Beautiful and peaceful countryside is a natural resource. It benefits the people who live there, but can attract too many visitors on vacation, over-using the resources.

i Have

Norway has so much oil and natural gas that it can export 50% of it. This makes up about a quarter of Norway's wealth, and its small population of 5 million people are able to live well.

The power of the wind can be harnessed to create energy.

The heat of the sun can be converted to electricity.

Some energy forms are natural. Hot steam pours from underground vents in Iceland.

i Don't Have

Greece, on the other hand, has very few natural resources. It has agricultural goods such as olive oil and fish. It has just enough to feed its 11 million population. As a result, Greece has to pay out to import other goods and its energy needs.

il

The largest and wealthiest industry in the world is oil production. This means everything to do with getting it out of the ground, refining or cleaning it, moving it through pipes or by tanker from place to place, and selling it to businesses and individuals who need it.

Wh⊛ needs it?

We all do! It's likely you use oil in the home – hundreds of times a day! Anything made of plastic started with oil, from the tips on your shoelaces to plastic cups and the bags at the supermarket.

Oil is also found in food preservatives, soap, bubble bath, and skin cream. Outside, it's in fertilizers, spray paint, and glue. And the family car can't move without gas – unless it's electric.

Why is it expensive?

Oil is a non-renewable energy source. That means quite simply that when we run out, there's no more left. And that's why it's precious. And valuable!

Earth provides us with plenty of natural resources that can be used as sources of energy. Those we've been using a lot in modern times are fossil fuels – coal, petroleum (crude oil), and natural gas.

Oil started as plants and tiny animals that lived in water hundreds of millions of years ago. Over these years, the remains of these animals were covered in sand and silt. Heat and pressure slowly turned them into oil, or petroleum. So the oil we use today cannot possibly be replaced.

Refined oil is stored in huge containers ready to be shipped or piped worldwide.

Crude oil, pumped from underground, is brought to the refinery where it is cleaned of impurities, bits of rock, and other materials.

Cars are the single largest users of gas.

OiL PUMPERS

Who has pumped out and exported the most oil?

* Russia
* Saudi Arabia
* United States
* Iran
* China
* Canada
* Iraq
* United Arab Emirates
* Venezuela
* Mexico

Car guzzlers

Oil has been used as a fuel, or energy source, for thousands of years. But when mass production of cars began at the beginning of the 20th century, oil was turned into gas to fuel them. Gas is now the main oil product.

INFLUENCES: Agriculture

Farming and growing produce is all part of an important industry called agriculture. At one time, it was the most important industry because it provided food for a country or food surpluses that could be traded for other things. Today, fewer people are involved in agriculture, but it's still as important an industry as it ever was.

Subsistence

Subsistence farming usually means growing things for your own use. A subsistence farm plants or raises only the crops and animals that the family will need. Little or nothing is left over to trade or sell.

However, many subsistence farmers try to trade surplus crops for things they can't grow, such as sugar, clothing, and iron roofing. Most subsistence farmers live in poor or developing countries in rural Africa and Asia. Some have developed trade contacts and links, selling items that use their specialized skills and local materials.

Surplus

When farmers grow crops mostly to sell, they sometimes produce more than they can get rid of. This is called a surplus. You might think that the best way to get rid of surplus wheat or butter would be to give it to countries with starving populations. But that doesn't work because it would lower the price of the commodity significantly and farmers would make little profit.

So what happens to the surplus? Sometimes it builds up and is left to rot. More likely it is 'dumped,' which means it's sold off cheaply.

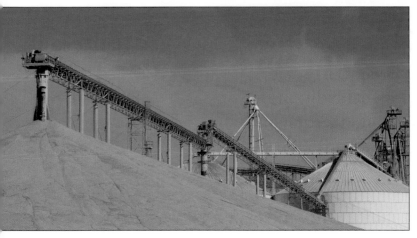

Surplus wheat is piled high.

Goods are transported using manpower.

A small catch must earn enough to feed the family.

Subsidies

From time to time, governments help out farmers by giving subsidies. A subsidy is some form of financial help. It may be made to encourage farmers to grow certain crops, or to encourage them not to and prevent a surplus from building up!

Fair Trade

Fair trade is a policy that helps poorer farmers in developing countries. It aims to make sure that those who produce commodities for sale abroad are not exploited or do not lose out through unfair trade and tariffs. The coffee and banana sectors are good examples.

Traditional farming methods in use.

Surplus foods are sold at the market.

INFLUENCES: Goods & Services

Industry usually means the manufacture, or making, of goods. In the 1700s and 1800s, new inventions made it possible to produce goods in large quantities and at lower cost. Factories sprang up, and countries that encouraged these industries became rich.

A conveyer belt carries goods from process to process by machine.

Making goods

Making goods provides work for a country's people. If the products are of high enough quality, the country gains a good reputation from selling both at home and abroad. Manufacturing also helps spread the money around, as factory workers spend their wages on different goods and services.

The basic materials

It's not necessarily easy to set up a manufacturing base. Most products are made from some kind of raw material. It's best if the raw materials come from the same country. If they have to be imported from another country, the costs will go up as well as the price of the finished product.

Specialists

With the right raw materials and the right kinds of workers, countries can become specialists at producing certain goods.

In the United States, the automobile industry became one specialist sector. Companies such as Ford and General Motors, produced cars for the American market as well as for export abroad. Now, both Japan and Korea have created a successful position in the automobile market. People all over the globe drive their cars.

In the United Kingdom, the major car players no longer manufacture. But small specialist carmakers have taken over, producing sports cars and other special cars.

Tourism

Countries that have lots of beautiful countryside or old cities and towns, historic sites, or some special or curious landmark, may get visited by people from other countries. People are always eager to travel to new places and see how others live.

Visitors from abroad, called tourists, need hotels. They need food and transportation. They pay to visit places and for entertainment. They spend their money in YOUR country. This is called the tourism industry, and in many countries it is a big, big service industry! Service industries do not manufacture goods - they provide services for people.

INFLUENCES: Goods & Services

As well as making things to sell, an economy also needs businesses that supply people with things such as tourism, banking, insurance, medical, or legal services. Service industries like these provide products that you can't easily see, but just like manufactured goods, they can earn lots of money for a country.

DEVELOPED COUNTRIES

Service industries are usually found in more developed countries in North America and Europe as well as Asian countries such as Singapore and South Korea. These all have a strong economy, good education, and a well-educated workforce.

A GROWING SECTOR

The service sector has grown steadily over the last hundred years. In the United States, for instance, it earned half the country's GDP in 1929. Fifty years later, it was earning two-thirds, and by 1993, more than three-quarters. Service industries now add up to more than three-fifths of the world's total earnings.

Mechanization

One reason that the service sector has grown so much is that manufacturing goods has become more and more mechanized. Machines, rather than people, now do much of the work. Fewer people are needed and so more emphasis is placed on the service jobs of distribution, advertising, management, and finance.

Office Workers

Governments have grown in size over the years. This means they need to employ more people. And government employees are all people involved in the service sector.

People who provide services generally work in offices. Sometimes their offices are at home.

Service industries

Here are some of the largest service industries around the world:

* Advertising
* Child care companies
* Entertainment
* Financial services
* Health care
* Hospitality - hotels and dining
* Insurance
* Legal services
* Marketing and sales
* Online services
* Tourism
* Travel

INFLUENCES: Neighbors

Peace

One of the things that stops a country from becoming wealthy is conflict, especially war. Apart from the destruction, wars stop countries from developing. Long periods of peace where countries trade and cooperate with each other, help growth and development.

Allies

Allies means friends. When countries have allies, they can trade with those allies and help the countries involved to grow their economies. Allies help each other by reducing special taxes known as tariffs and making trade easier.

Wars cost money

One of the worst disasters happened in 2000 when the country of Ethiopia was at war with its neighbor Eritrea. Millions of dollars were spent on soldiers and military equipment that could have been used to reduce the people's poverty.

Working together

Sometimes countries find it easier to work together to become wealthier. They may form unions that use the same currency. Borders are easier to cross, which makes importing and exporting easier.

INFLUENCES: Education

in School

From the day a child starts school, parents try to give them the best education they can. They know that the better educated they are, the more likely they are to get a well-paid job and lead a more fulfilling life.

Education starts at an early age.

Literacy

Literacy means being able to read and write. Most countries of the world try to educate their population so that each individual can develop their knowledge and achieve their goals in life. High literacy rates are enjoyed in all industrial countries, but of the larger countries, only Norway can boast a 100% literacy level. Poor literacy holds countries back – in Afghanistan, for example, 43% of the men are literate, but only 12.6% of the women are. This limits how mothers can help and encourage their children with learning.

Many children will spend 12 or more years in school.

Graduating from school helps to get a good job.

High-Low earners

The more you can earn, the better off your country becomes. A country that produces lots of high earners such as engineers, computer programmers, doctors, and so on, is almost certainly going to have a high GDP. A country in which most people have just a primary school education or where wealth may be based on family farming, will probably have a lower GDP.

INFLUENCES: Labor

In many countries, the economy works because of its workforce. This term describes the people who live and work there, their skills, and the jobs they do to earn money.

The WORKFORCE

In many countries, people work from the time they leave school or college, or some form of training, until they reach retirement age. They will have worked for 40 years or more, and they stop at that point to enjoy their later life.

Once educated and trained, workers give their skills to many different kinds of jobs. If businesses are succeeding, even growing, more people will be employed. Their earnings are used to buy things, and this keeps money moving through stores, offices, and factories, and the whole economy is active.

WORK ethic

Some countries are known for the hard work their workers do. People are willing to work hard both for themselves and for the good of their country. We say they have a strong work ethic. Countries with this kind of attitude among the workforce tend to have the fastest-growing economies.

Training

Almost every job needs some form of training after education ends. It may take years before a person is fully trained and can contribute.

labor market

A country may have a large workforce – lots of people able to work for a living – but they may not have the right skills or live close to where the jobs are, or may not be willing to do the jobs that are available.

Cities attract a large workforce and the labor market operates freely.

The term 'labor market' describes how employees – willing workers – and employers – the people who wish to employ them – come together to produce something. They agree what the job is, where and how long the work will be done, and how much pay or other reward there will be.

Some jobs require the skills of a whole team.

Cheaper-Faster

Some countries are short of people to perform certain skills and jobs. Perhaps these jobs are repetitive and boring. Maybe the wages aren't very high. So employers need to import labor from another country to help out. Or they employ the same people abroad and import the finished goods.

In some countries, young people must work long hours at repetitive jobs and for little money. They do not go to school.

Child labor

It's a sad fact that some countries have many young people with little or no education. Here, company bosses employ them to do unskilled and often dangerous work, with long hours and little pay. This is known as child labor, and it is a world problem.

INFLUENCES: Population

The total number of people living in a country is known as its population. In most countries, the birth of each child and the death of each family member must be recorded with the authorities. So the population figure is generally accurate.

UP AND DOWN

The world population is the total number of living humans on Earth. Today, it is estimated to be over 7.1 billion people. The numbers have grown steadily since the 1300s, with the fastest growth during the 1950 to 1960s. But since 1963, the rate of growth has slowed. However, there is still a worry that the planet will not have enough water, food, and energy resources for all.

OVER a billion ...

China was worried that its population was growing too fast. So in 1979, it passed a law forbidding couples to have more than one child. There were exceptions, but most people had to obey the law or face a heavy fine. Today, the law has been modified and many Chinese couples can have more than one child.

young world

Just over a quarter of the world's population is aged under 15. In another 10 years, they will be the workforce. But will there be too many people on the planet by then – or not enough?

The size of families is declining worldwide due to higher living standards and better work opportunities for women. In Japan, for example, this is seen as a real problem. For the 3rd year running, Japan has reported a low birth rate which does not replace the population that is dying. There are now far more elderly people than young ones. Soon there will be fewer workers and fewer consumers to keep the economy going.

A large, young population is a healthy sign for a country's economy.

MOST POPULATED COUNTRIES
(people in billions and millions)

* 1 China   1,364,600,000
* 2 India   1,244,430,000
* 3 United States   318,087,000
* 4 Indonesia   247,424,598
* 5 Brazil   202,598,000
* 6 Pakistan   186,527,000
* 7 Nigeria   173,615,000
* 8 Bangladesh   152,518,015
* 9 Russia   143,700,000
* 10 Japan   127,100,000

The cost of caring for the elderly comes from the tax contribution of the younger workforce.

INFLUENCES: Technology

It's easy to forget that using the computer as a daily tool is a new thing. Your grandparents watched TV on a solid, boxed screen, at first in black and white only. You'd go crazy if you were asked to do the same!

Communications

Communications, as we know it, are very recent. Only a few hundred years ago, if you wanted to tell somebody something, you had to write a letter. You could only find out what was going on in the world through talking or reading a newspaper – that's if you could read. But with the development of electricity, everything began to change.

Skilled workers assemble high-tech equipment.

Space technology opens up new communication methods.

Now, in our world of advanced technology, everyone can be in touch with just the click of a button. And this has changed the way people work and the way countries make their money.

Computers can design holographic buildings for architects.

keeping up

Countries at the forefront of the technology revolution have done well.

That's because there is a worldwide demand for technology such as computers and mobile phones. Some Asian countries lead the world in the production and manufacture of electronic technology. Your phone may have been bought at home, but it was probably made in China, Korea, or Japan.

Losing Out

Countries that don't have a technology base tend to lose out. They have to import gadgets, and that means money moves out of their country and into the country of manufacture. We are also in a period of great change in the way we communicate, and this means changing the way we teach skills. Countries that provide high-tech education create a useful workforce for the technology industry. Those that don't may lose out.

Creativity

Every invention that has ever been dreamed up has come from the brain of a truly creative person. Creativity is where new ideas are born.

Today, in a world where there is a lot of competition and rivalry between companies, someone who has a fresh approach to problems – a person who can "think outside the box" – is welcome in many innovative companies.

Creativity comes with knowledge. If you understand science or math or geography or economics or your chosen subject really well you are more likely to be an inventor of the future.

Trading With Other Countries

Most countries tend to concentrate on producing goods and services that they can make better or cheaper than other countries. If they make more than they need themselves, they can then trade the surplus with other nations.

EXP★RtS

Exports are goods and services that are supplied to and bought by companies or governments in other countries. Exporting, or selling goods abroad, is good for a country because it brings cash in and creates wealth.

iMP★RtS

Goods and services that are brought into a country to sell are called imports. Imports cost nations money because the company that imports them has to pay for them. So, money moves out of the country.

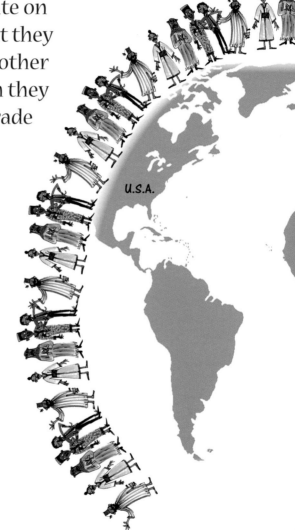

U.S.A.

T★P iMP★RteR

The U.S. imports more than any other country.

TOP EXPORTER
China exports more than any other country.

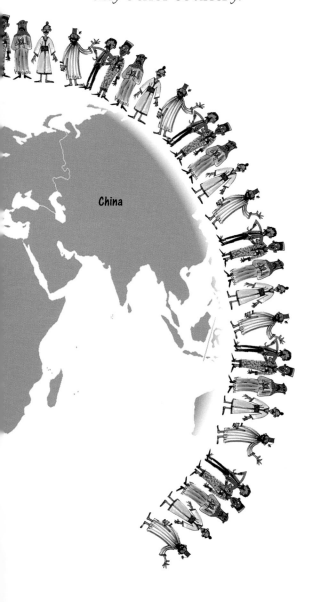

China

Keeping a balance

A country's trade balance is about what the country has sold abroad and what it has bought from abroad.

The difference between what a country buys and what it sells is the trade gap.

However, most countries don't want a big gap between what they buy and what they sell. They try to find a balance, known as a trade balance, between their exports and their imports. So when they export a great deal, they also tend to import a great deal as well.

To Help or Not to Help

Many people think that governments should not interfere too much in the economy of a country. They believe that business people know what they are doing and know how to make money.

Free to trade

Those who support working in a free market say that when a government interferes too much, businesses don't work well. Business owners should be able to decide themselves how much to pay their workers and how much they can export – in fact, how to run their own businesses.

They say business owners will lose interest in growing their business if they can't make the maximum profit.

Controls on trade

Other people believe that governments should be involved in business and that they can help.

In this way, governments make rules that businesses have to stand by. Among other things, they can introduce rules to help their own country's trade and to stop other countries from taking this business. They do this by interfering in the free market. They create barriers to hinder competition. These are known as trade barriers.

Barriers

A trade barrier is anything that hinders trade.

Tariffs are special taxes on imported goods that make them more expensive. The purpose of the tariff is to make domestic goods cheaper than the imported ones.

Quotas limit the amount of imported goods that can enter a country within a certain period of time. Of course, domestic companies have no such limits.

Product standards can also be used as a barrier to trade. For example, some countries do not permit the import of genetically altered (GM) beef or wheat. This protects local farmers from competition, too.

A stable government

In some countries, the government changes often. In others, the government remains in place for a fixed term, say four years.

If the government is involved in how businesses run and create wealth for the country, it doesn't help if they keep changing. Changing governments might introduce new rules and regulations just when a business is getting used to the old ones. So, stable governments – ones that stay around for a fixed period – are better for business.

Your Part to Play

Wherever you live, you'll be expected to contribute to your country's economy once you are an adult. Whether you work as a lawyer, a nurse, a cab driver – or whatever, you're going to be part of what makes your country wealthy.

Getting Educated

It starts with your education. Most developed countries offer free education at least through the high school level. Governments control the education system to make sure young people have the basic skills to make their way in life, such as the ability to read or do basic mathematics and computer operations.

Higher education prepares students in more specialized ways. A university degree may prepare you for a professional career, while a technical school might prepare you to enter an industry.

Choosing a Career

You may be good at something from an early age that points you in the direction of a particular career. If you're really good at math, for instance, you might want to train as a teacher or get a degree in physics, which might lead you to a career in astronomy. If you're not sure which career you want to choose, there are career instructors in schools to help you.

Getting Trained

Your education may not end with school. Training in specialist skills is often carried out in the workplace. Companies may offer apprenticeships where you can learn a trade while you work. Other agencies also offer training courses to help with basic skills.

Location

There are places in many countries where specific jobs are carried out. The technology sector is big in an area of California called 'Silicon Valley,' for instance. The financial sector thrives in one area of London called 'The City,' If you want to do the job you're trained for, you may have to move to where the job exists.

Today, populations are more mobile, and people are more willing to go to the right place for them. Mobility helps the economy, although some people would argue that one area's success means another area's failure and that work opportunities should be more evenly spread.

Your Contribution

Once you're working, you're contributing to the economy. You do this through the taxes you pay and the money you spend. Whether you're buying a new car, a house, or food to eat, you're putting money into the economy that allows other people to thrive and contribute as well.

And it doesn't matter what you do or how much you earn – once you are working, you are helping the economy to grow and your country to prosper.

Let's Discuss This!

is taxation fair?

All countries have to raise money, so most apply taxes to their working population. Different countries ask for different amounts. And usually, the more you earn, the more you have to pay. Is it fair to tax the rich more heavily than low-paid workers? Or should everyone pay the same amount regardless of how much they earn?

Printing Money

Does printing money solve financial problems? Countries are responsible for printing their money. They can print as much as they want to. So if a country gets into financial trouble, why not just print more bills?

What's your currency like?

Could you come up with a better design? Whose head would you have on YOUR currency? What colors and what pattern would you use?

is inflation a bad thing?

Inflation means rising prices. Some economists argue that a small amount of inflation is not a bad thing. Others say that inflation has to be kept low or removed altogether. Why is inflation considered to be bad for an economy?

is child labor justified?

In some countries, children work long hours for low pay. This may help keep costs down, make products competitive, and boost the economy. But can child labor anywhere be considered acceptable?

What does your country export?

Exporting goods or services can help a country's economy grow. Countries that can produce goods more cheaply than others will do well. But that might mean low wages and poor working conditions. Is that the right way to go? What goods or services does your country export?

Additional Resources

BOOKS

Canino, Rose. *How Trade Deficits Work*. New York, New York:
Rosen Publishing Company, 2012.

Duignan, Brian,ed. *Banking and Finance*. Chicago, Illinois:
Britannica Educational Publishers, 2013.

Furgang, Kathy. *Understanding Budget Deficits and the National Debt*.
New York, New York: Rosen Publishing Company, 2012.

Websites

Kids.gov
www.kids.usa.gov/money/index.shtml
This site provides all kinds of information about money.

U.S. Mint for Kids
www.usmint.gov/kids
Learn all about the history of money in the United States, watch
cartoons about coins, or join the collector's club.

Glossary

birth rate
The rate at which a country can measure and compare the number of babies born in a given period of time.

budget deficit
The difference between what a country needs to pay for all its obligations and the money it has available to do so.

commodities
The name given to essential products such as grains and metals, that are bought and sold in large quantities.

communications
A general term that describes ways in which people pass information to each other using modern technology.

consumer spending
A description of how people spend their money and how much they spend.

crash
A sudden and dramatic drop in a market's value.

debt
Borrowed money to be repaid.

democracies
A system of running countries in which the people who live there choose their leaders.

economy
The financial and business activity of a country.

exporting
Selling goods and services abroad to earn money.

fossil fuels
Fuels such as coal and oil that are found in Earth, where they have developed over millions of years.

free market
A way an economy can work in which businesses are free to operate as they please with no government rules.

governments
Groups of people elected to run a country on behalf of its people.

Gross Domestic Product
The total earnings of a country. This is often referred to as GDP.

healthcare program
A government-run program that makes sure all people receive some form of medical care.

importing
To buy goods and services from a foreign country.

income
Another name for earnings.

income tax
A tax paid to the government by people who earn wages.

inflation
The way in which money loses value and buys less as the cost of goods and services rises.

investment
Money lent to a person or company to
help it trade.

literacy
The ability to read and write.

natural resources
Something that is naturally available
in an environment, such as water or oil
or forests. A workforce is also a natural
resource.

poverty
The state of not having enough money
for basic needs.

quotas
Restrictions set by a government
on how much of something can be
imported or exported.

raw materials
A material such as timber or metal,
which can be turned into some
other product.

services
Activities such as schools and museums
that are paid for by local governments.

subsidies
A government payment made to help a
business or service.

surplus
Extra goods that are not used
locally and which may not be
needed abroad either.

tariffs
Taxes set by the government
of a country to make imports
more expensive.

taxes
A part of income or payments, collected
by governments for general use.

tax havens
Countries that set very low, or even no
tax levels.

wages
Money earned on a regular basis in
exchange for work.

work ethic
The desire to work hard for a living.

workforce
The people who work in a country
or a business.

Index